Kate and Suki like to play.

puzzle

draw

Help Tom and Kate to get to school.

read

match

write

your	school	_____
just	wait	_____
with	just	just
school	do	_____
sand	your	_____
wait	with	_____
do	sand	_____

read   write

tree   trees

_____   balls

_____   books

rabbit   _____

boat   _____

_____   beds

_____   dogs

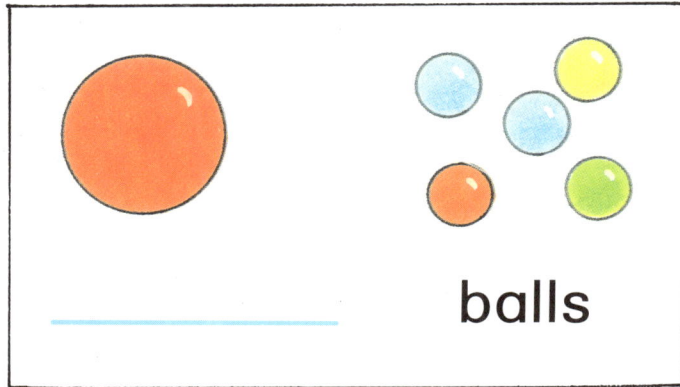

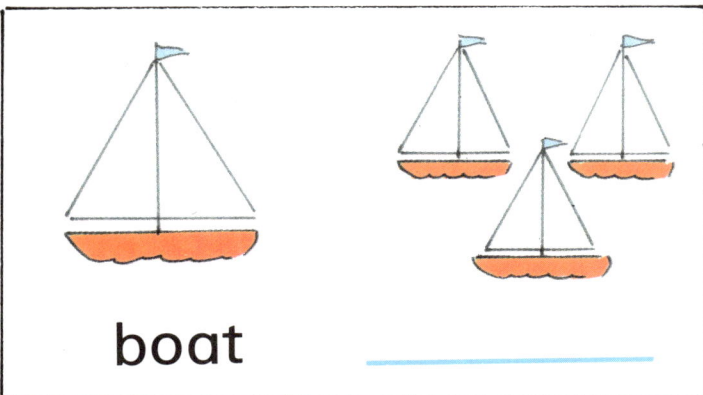

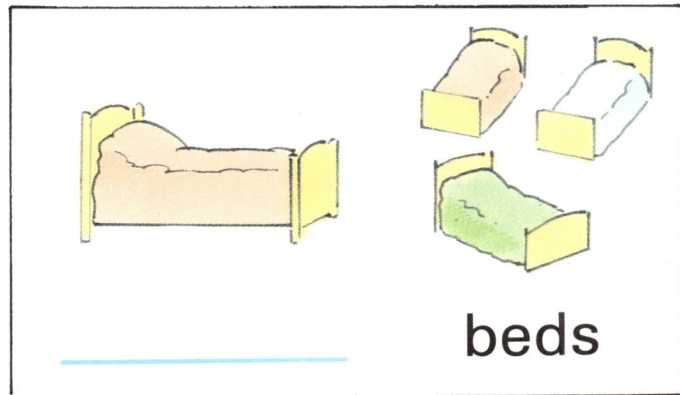

Fill in the missing words.

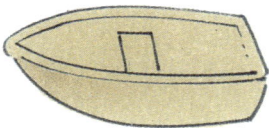

bed

mother

lunch box

Suki

book

rabbit

Tom

boat

fish

hat

Kate

sand

tree

Sam

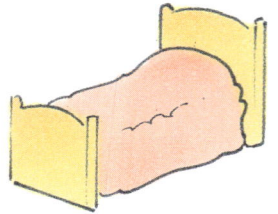

Colour the odd one out in each row.

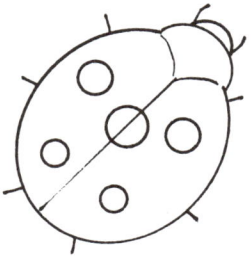

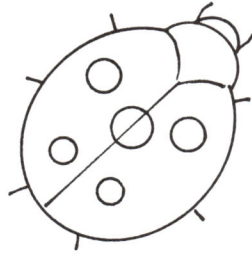

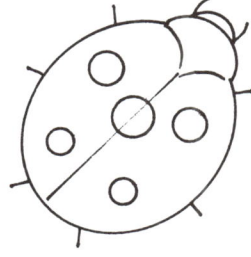

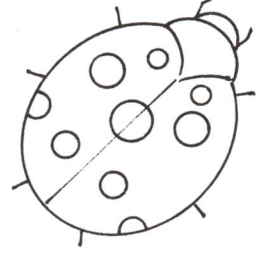

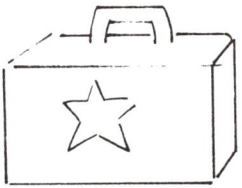

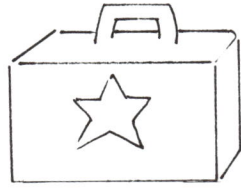

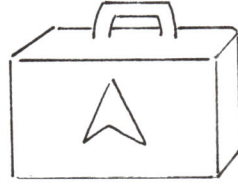

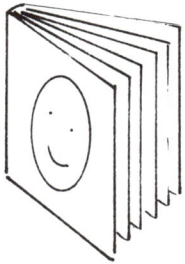

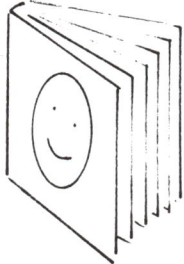

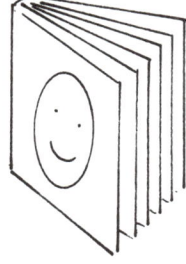

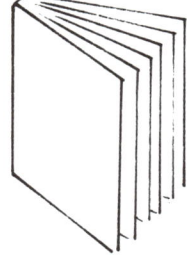

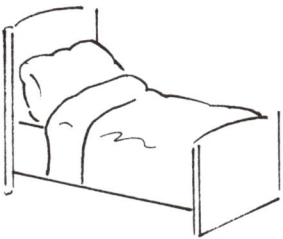

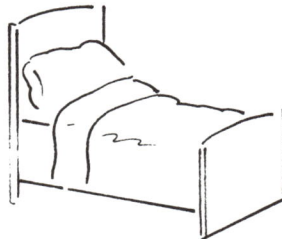

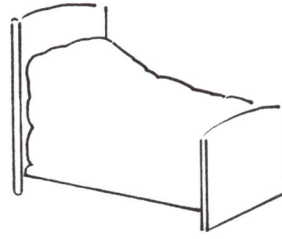

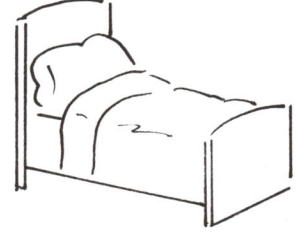

 read  write

Tick the correct box.

Sam has a ball.

yes ☐
no ☐

Is this Kate's hat?

yes ☐
no ☐

Kate plays with the sand.

yes ☐
no ☐

Can Sam jump?

yes ☐
no ☐

Tom has a rabbit.

yes ☐
no ☐

puzzle draw colour

Finish each row.

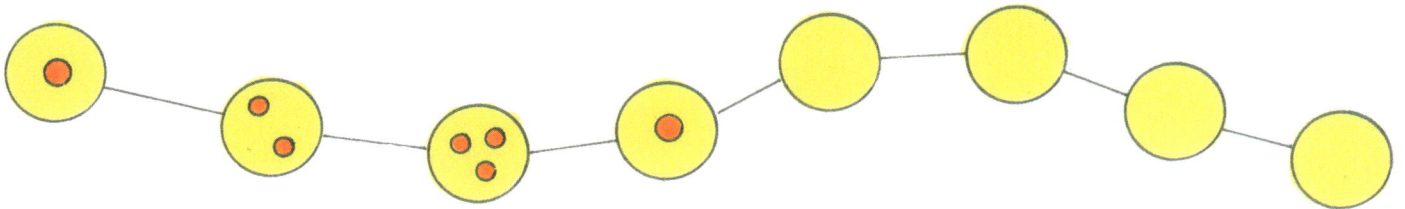

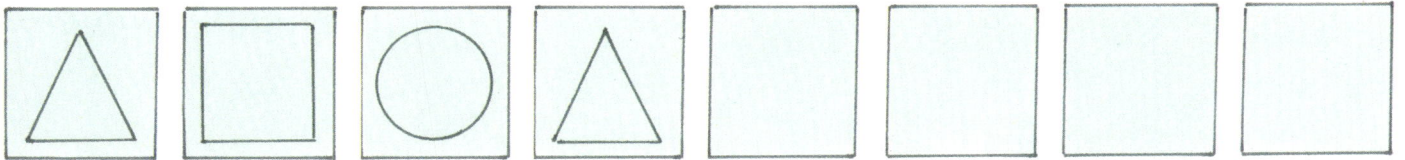

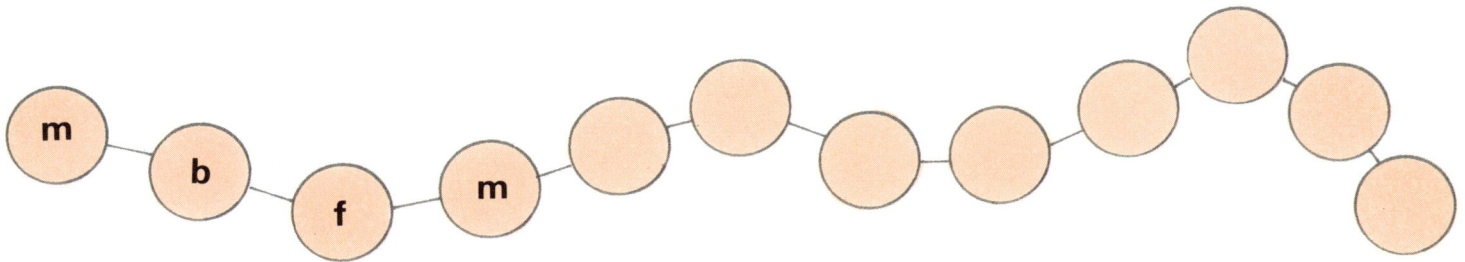

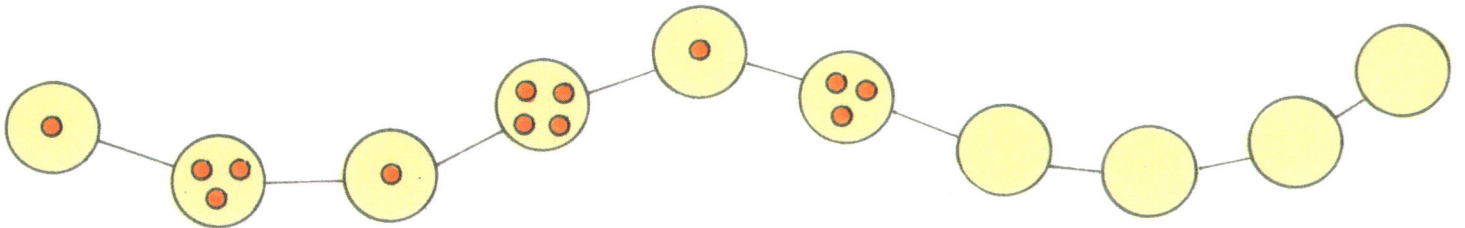

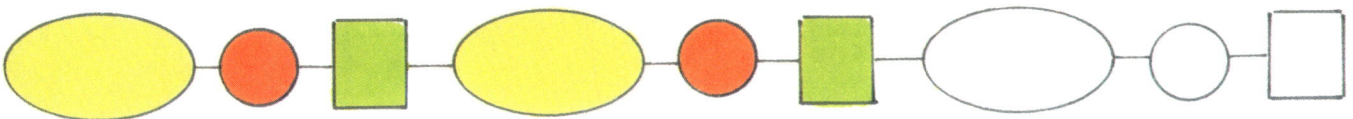

 read
 write

Fill in the missing words.

Here is the _____.

    (school, teacher, fish)

Tom says, Sam can't have the _____.

    (hat, must, put)

I want this toy, _____.

    (come, yours, please)

Kate and Suki make a _____.

    (water, fish, please)

They can go _____ in the water.

    (read, please, round)

This fish can _____ in the water.

    (stay, over, now)

 puzzle
 draw

Help the mouse to find the cheese.

 read
 match
 write

stay	must _____
over	read _____
come	that _____
must	now _____
now	come _____
read	stay *stay*
that	over _____

Colour the two which are the same as the first one in each row.

 read  write

Fill in the missing words.

ball   hat   lunch box
book   rabbit   Kate   Sam

Suki has her _____.

The _____ can play.

Tom can read the _____.

I can see _____ jump.

This _____ is round.

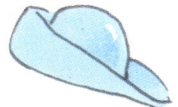

Put this _____ on, please.

The teacher tells _____ to come now.

Help Suki to colour her rainbow.

r o y g b i v

r **o** **y** **g** **b** **i** **v**

red   yellow   blue   violet

orange   green   indigo

Cut out the sixteen cards and use them to play reading and matching games. These cards can be added to those from Activity Books 1 and 3.

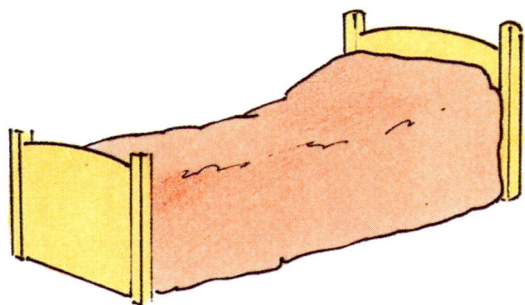

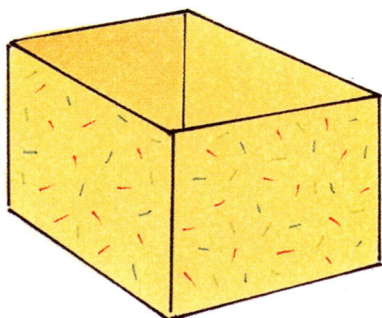

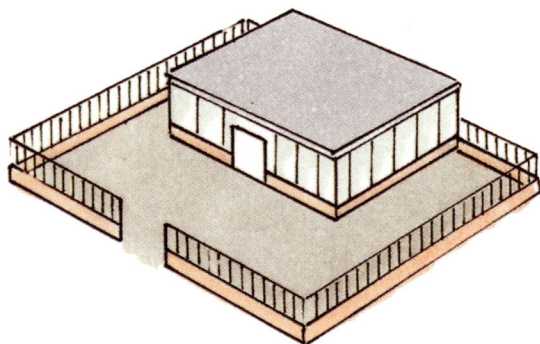

You can match a word with a word, a picture with a picture or a word with a picture.

book	bed
mother	box
sand	rabbit
read	school

Play snap with a partner or lay down all the picture cards and ask your partner to match the correct word.

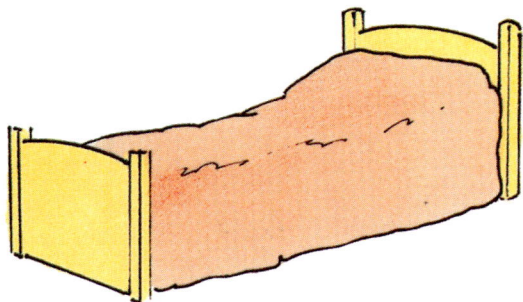

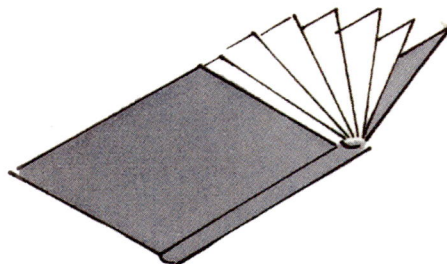

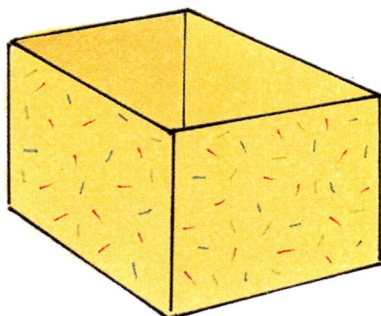

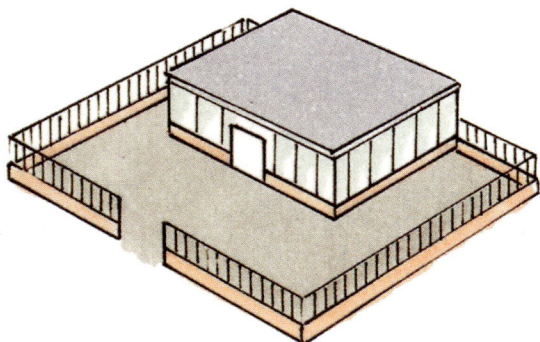

book	bed
mother	box
sand	rabbit
read	school

 read
 write

Tom likes to _____.
(must, boats, read)

Can you see this
_____, Suki says.
(play, fish, round)

They play with
the _____.
(toys, round, please)

I can put Tom's
rabbit _____.
(over, now, here)

puzzle	read	match					

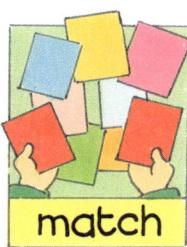

Find the hidden words.
You can go across or down.

toy
book
sand
box
bed
rabbit
school
read
play
fish
boy

a	c	t	d	e	f	g	s
b	o	o	k	v	i	l	c
o	x	y	m	r	s	b	h
x	n	f	g	e	h	e	o
y	z	p	s	a	n	d	o
h	t	l	s	d	r	k	l
s	r	a	b	b	i	t	y
b	o	y	t	q	u	r	v

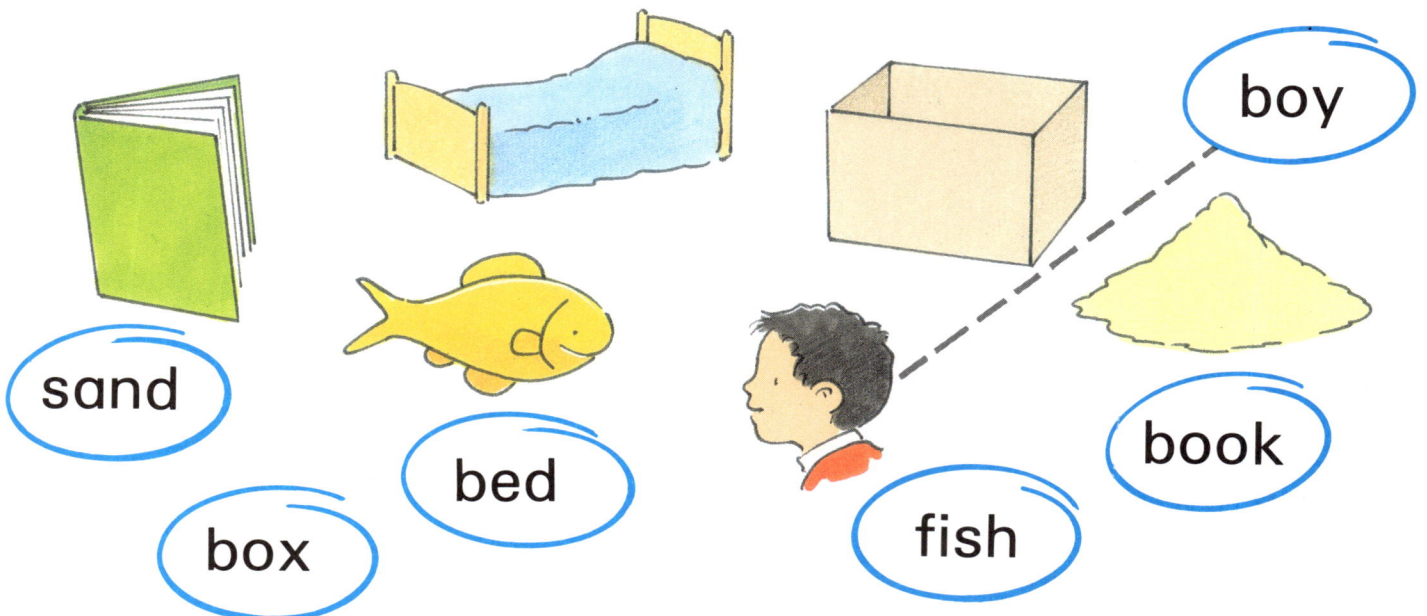

boy

sand

book

box

bed

fish

Draw a line to join the word to the picture.

read | write

Write the correct word under each picture.

sand   toy   book   Suki   lunch box   teacher

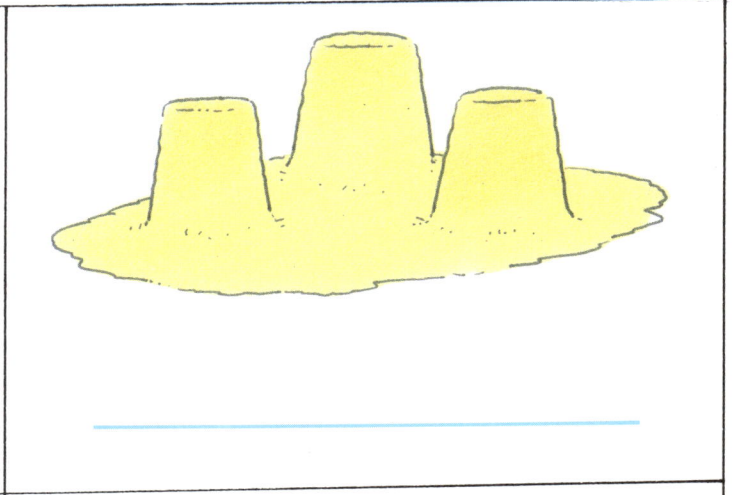

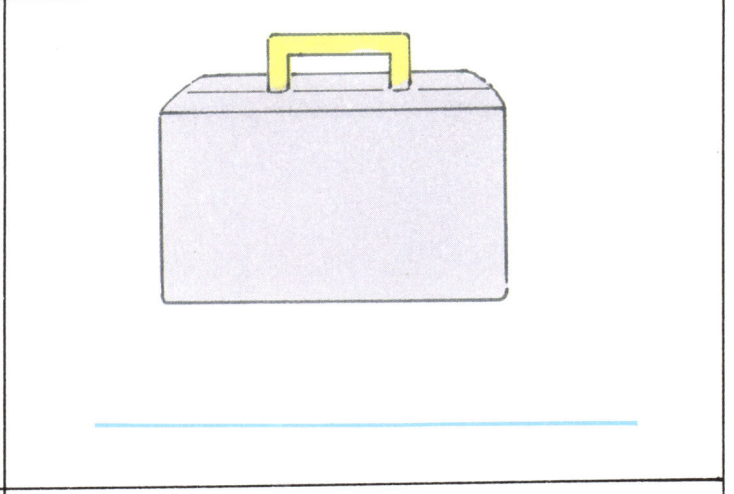

_____

_____

_____

_____

_____

_____

Draw a line to join the correct storybook characters together.

Colour the shapes that have a dot to see the picture.

We can do this,

say Kate and Suki.

Match the sentences to the correct picture.

They can run. Sam can run faster.

They go home. There they all go.

Give it to me, she says.

talk

Tell the story.

Colour those that are the same as the first one in each row.

How many crocodiles can you find in the picture?

What might happen next?

Make up a story.

For each row, put the pictures in the right order to tell the story.

A crocodile collage

Draw a shape like this on a large piece of paper or left-over strip of wallpaper.

From old magazines, cut or tear small pieces of pictures with green, brown or yellow colours.

Mix up your coloured pieces and paste them onto your crocodile shape. Add a silver foil eye and white teeth cut from white paper.

Kate and Suki
can do this.